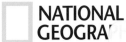

NATIONAL
GEOGRAPHIC

T0058646

What is
the Pattern?

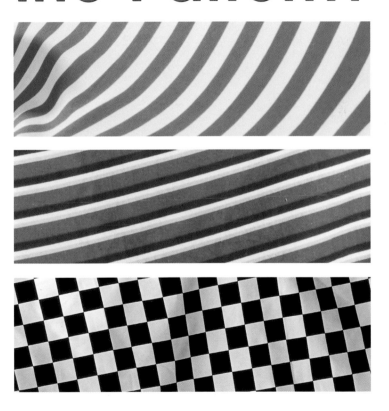

Jan Pritchett

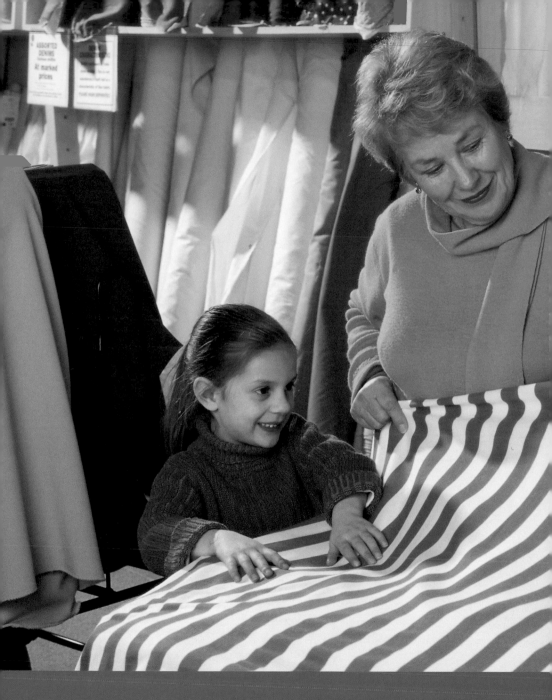

2   What is the pattern?

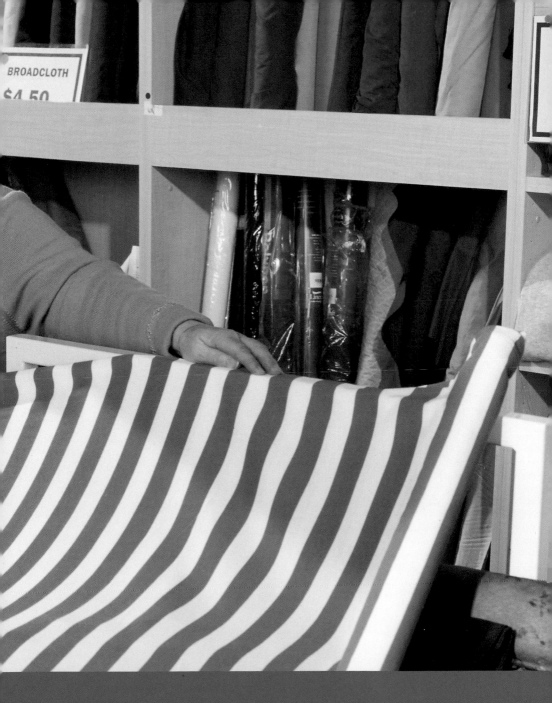

BROADCLOTH
$4.50

3

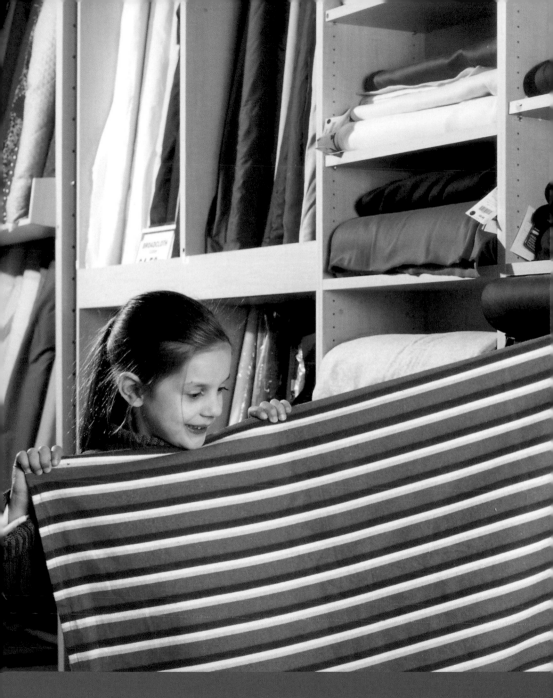

4   What is the pattern?

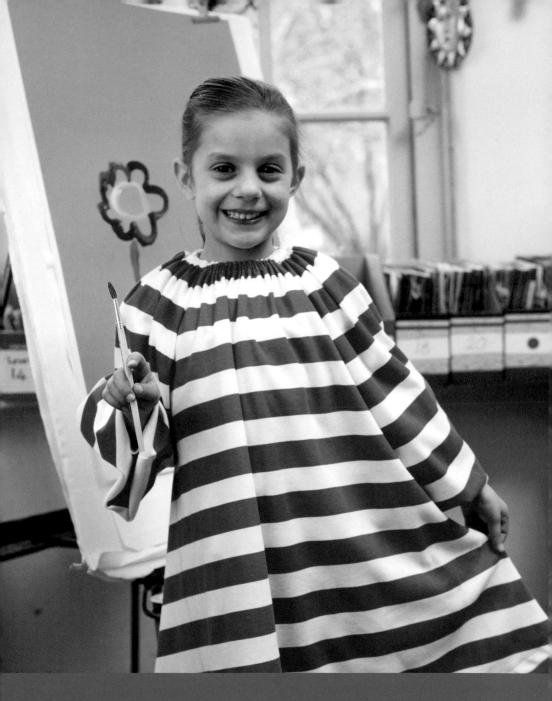

8   I like this pattern!

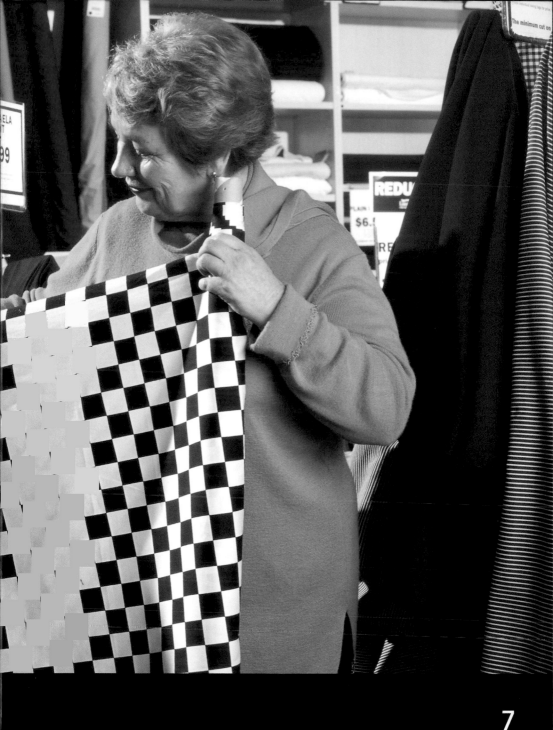

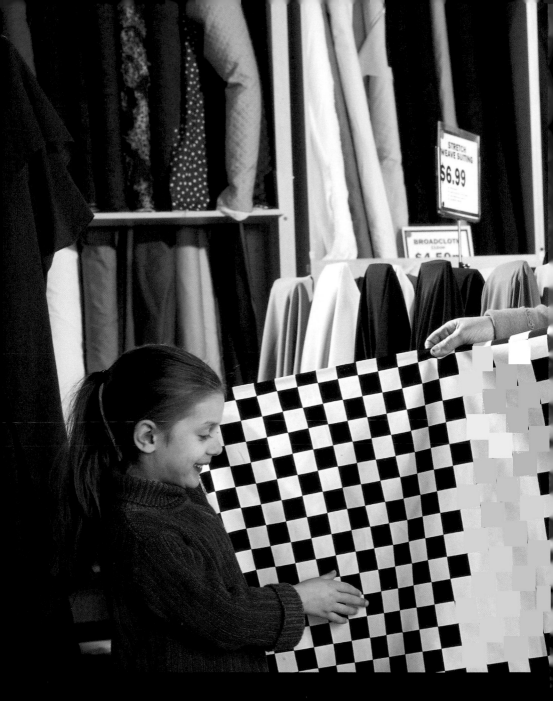

STRETCH
WEAVE SUITING

$6.99

BROADCLOTH

$4.50

6   What is the pattern?

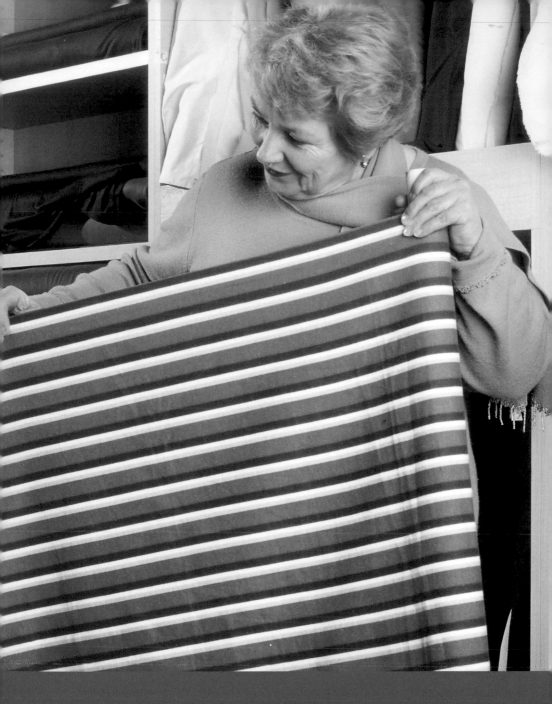